BIJOU
Bijou

 Published in the United States of America by Green Pieces, LLC. For information, write Green Pieces Cartoon Studio Press, 7904 E. Chaparral Road, #A110-496, Scottsdale, AZ 85250-7210.

http://www.pierre-orourke.com; http://www.greenpiecesbooks.com; mail@greenpiecestoons.com

GREEN PIECES PRESS
Scottsdale, Arizona
www.GreenPiecesBooks.com

Publisher's Cataloging-in-Publication Data

O'Rourke, Pierre.

Note to Gibbs / by Pierre O'Rourke ; illustrated and cartoons by Drew Aquilina.
-- 1st ed. -- Scottsdale, AZ : Green Pieces Press, c2014.

p. ; cm.

ISBN: 978-0-9860580-8-0 (print); 978-0-9860580-4-2 (ebook)
Summary: A humorous guide to and observation of the real
day-to-day joy of raising and training a puppy.

1. Dogs--Humor. 2. Dogs--Training--Humor. 3. Puppies--Humor.
4. Puppies--Training--Humor. 5. Pets--Humor. 6. Pets--Caricatures and cartoons.
7. Human-animal relationships--Humor. 8. Humorous fiction.
9. Comic books, strips, etc. I. Aquilina, Drew. II. Title.

PN6231.D68 O76 2014
636.7/08870202--dc23 1402

Covers designed and drawn by Drew Aquilina

For Nubble

You taught me even more about unguarded love and unconditional love.

You were my first co-pilot as I took the leap to becoming an author.

You would have liked Gibbs ...

in fact, I believe that spot on his side is your paw print from picking him out for me.

I miss you, Fur-Face.

Acknowledgments

I owe thanks to many in making *Note to Gibbs* a reality.

Janet Jorgenson and Canine Village Rescue & Dog Hotel for lovingly and gently determining that 'Ernest Hemingstray' belonged with an author. Pat and Duffy McMahon for prodding me to check out this puppy, and later nudging me to turn the notes into a book. Erin Rose Bunzel for figuring her dad is a much better dad when there is a dog involved. Bijou for paw-selecting my pup, helping raise him, and being his best friend and soul mate.

Shay Wheeler & Chelsea Stansell did such a great job fostering 'Ernest' before the adoption. Louisc Lopcz and Arizona Cattle Dog Rescue for seeing the beauty in him when, from a litter of six, his silly breeders saw him as "'miscolored' with big feet."

Duffy also gets credit for being my virtual partner from Day 1 on this book and the concept. She made it happen. Drew Aquilina for taking the notes and magically making them visual with his cartoons. Green Pieces Press Publishing and Lisa Aquilina for her faith, guidance, and keeping writing fun.

Rosemary Scarfo and Laura Holka for sorting through over 700 notes. Judy Worman began as my editor, morphing into Nubble's and now Gibbs' aunt who dog-sits the very few times he is not with me. Sherry Hays is another aunt, phenomenal researcher, plus helps me keep the mounting notes organized. Edward Ellsworth is my webmaster extraordinaire and designer of my websites. Valerie Moore keeps an eye on Edward, and their pups Lily and Molly when not line-editing my novels.

Lisa Gardner and Deborah Coonts for support and advice with my writing while honoring Nubble and adopting Gibbs. Andrew Grant and Xander and Tasha Alexander for merely being who they are and for my Nubble Zen Garden. Joan Parker for taking over for Bob as my mentor. Boston and the world will never be the same.

Jeff Curl for friendship and movie time. Dr. Dick Stolper and Scottsdale Ranch Animal Hospital for keeping Gibbs healthy. Chelsie Laws of Murad, Inc. and Dr. Joseph Lillo for keeping me healthy. Regina Jones and Shampooch Salon for beautifying Bijou and 'handsome-fying' Gibbs. Partners Dog Training has helped me have the best of two and now three dogs. Dr. Marty Becker & The Bond, my writing buddy and Gibbs' long-distance vet and uncle.

Denise, Ken and Wylie of Rehab Burger Therapy - Chris Pease & Chelsea's Kitchen – Monte and Starbucks on Hayden - all for helping train Gibbs in restaurant manners.

Gino Ater, Joanie Blunt, Ralph Bradshaw, Kathy Brady, Charlene Centoz, Jannelle Combs, Rita Davenport, Daniel Lewis, Corrina Pfaff, Dave Pratt, Chuck Schrader & Family, Karen and Howard Smolin, Shandaé and Joel Erik Thompson, Bobby Worman, Jim Worman and Jami Fowler and their dogs Porter and Karma, Chris Zimmerman, Tim and Lori Zunk and Archangel Gabriel for keeping all hours. Also the faith and support given by those who dare to dream at Kickstarter. As Michael Landon used to say, "Here's to the Dreamers."

Gibbs and I send hugs and wags to you all.

Meet the Author, Pierre O'Rourke

Pierre O'Rourke has worked as an artist, cartoonist, publicist, forest firefighter, landscaper, celebrity contact, producer, interviewer, columnist, emcee, actor, movie critic, maitre d', and media host to authors and celebrities along his journey figuring out what he wants to be when he grows up.

His prior company, Celebrity Promotions, put him in direct contact with celebrities and authors. For fifteen years, he produced celebrity events such as tennis and golf tournaments, silent auctions, poker rides, skeet shoots and rodeos to raise money for charities. O'Rourke continues to assist personalities in promoting their book releases, film productions and projects in Arizona by serving as a Media Host to Authors when the authors are on publicity tours in Arizona.

Authors such as Og Mandino, John Lescroart, Rita Mae Brown, Robert B. Parker, Lee Child and various celebrities including Michael Landon, Buddy Ebsen, Willie Nelson, Johnny Cash and many others with whom he worked over the years, urged O'Rourke to begin writing his own books. It only took him twelve years to listen and take action.

Free the Puddles was completed in November 2011 as an eBook. *Note To Gibbs* will be followed by *Dog Gone! The Fire Hydrant-Way to Heaven*, an unrelated novel involving God and his best friend, Shadow.

Additionally, O'Rourke is completing *Driving Me Crazy*, the second of his Daro Brónach novels. That story begins in Scottsdale where O'Rourke often can be found on patios writing with Gibbs at his side. Neither have plans of growing up anytime soon.

Meet the Cartoonist, Drew Aquilina

International award-winning cartoonist and best-selling author Drew Aquilina has been entertaining audiences nationwide for years. A Connecticut native, Aquilina graduated from UMass Amherst with a Bachelor of Science degree in Landscape Architecture while creating the cartoon strip *Green Pieces*©. The strip was copyrighted and ran as a daily and weekly feature in three Connecticut newspapers, various East Coast newspapers and other University student publications in Connecticut and Arizona as a daily and weekly comic feature from 1994 to present, as well as a daily online cartoon strip since 2008.

Aquilina's 2011 debut cartoon compilation, *Green Pieces: Green From the Pond Up* has sold over 100,000 copies worldwide and was named Comics/Graphic Novel of the Year at the London, Paris, New York, New England, San Francisco and Green Book Festivals. Aquilina's inaugural publication also was named USA "Best Books 2011" Awards-Environment/Green Book of the Year and was awarded the Humor Finalist distinction at the 2012 IBPA Benjamin Franklin Awards, the National Indie Excellence Awards and the Next Generation Indie Book Awards. Who knew being green could be so hilarious?

Aquilina is the staff cartoonist at AZTV Channel 7/Cable 13 in Phoenix, AZ and is an accomplished national cartoonist instructor and humorist speaker. Aquilina continues to produce a daily Green Pieces strip at http://www.GreenPiecesCartoons.com and http://www.GoComics.com/green-pieces. The release of his fourth cartoon book, *The Fifth World: Rise of Two Kingdom*s, is due to be released in March 2014, as Aquilina continues his quest to become nationally syndicated.

A Registered Landscape Architect in Arizona, California and Nevada, Aquilina lives in Paradise Valley, AZ with his wife, Lisa, and their own version of Green Pieces. Follow Aquilina and Green Pieces on Facebook at https://www.facebook.com/greenpiecestoons and on Twitter at: @greenpiecesbook http://twitter.com/greenpiecesbook.

eBook by PIERRE O'ROURKE

Free the Puddles

PIERRE O'ROURKE as a Contributing Author

The Ultimate Dog Lover by Dr. Marty Becker

The Ultimate Christian by Todd Outcalt

Note to Gibbs: The Beginning

We operate under the illusion that our dogs and cats will be our lifelong friends. The reality is that we are given the choice and honor of being *their* lifelong friends (and I choose to believe we will be reunited one day). It is a fearful thing to love what death can touch. At times reality bites.

Nubble had been my canine buddy since he was eight weeks old. Many have read stories of my exploits with this rescued Aussie Cattle Herder / Border mix. Nubble was befriended by Bijou, one of my closest friend's Goldendoodle. Over ten years later, it abruptly became time to make a most dreaded decision and Nubble was gone. I had a huge hole in my heart.

One and one-half years passed before I braved another dog. Another rescued Aussie Herder entered my life. Janet Jorgensen of Canine Village Rescue sent me pictures of a puppy named 'Ernest Heminstray.' Ernest was in doggie foster care and Janet figured he should find a permanent home with an author. While I found the pictures to be cute, I told Janet, "No thanks. Not ready." At dinner with my daughter Erin and dear friends Pat and Duffy McMahon, I was quizzed as to why I turned down 'Ernest.' Duffy asked, "Have you asked for a sign from Nubble?" I replied I had done so but received nothing. My outspoken and wise daughter quipped, "He sent you a frigging puppy; what more do you want?"

Three days later, Duffy, Bijou and I made the long drive to meet Ernest. I had gathered a few potential names to replace 'Ernest,' such as 'Parker' or 'Spenser' to honor my former mentor Robert B. Parker, or perhaps 'Reacher' in admiration of Lee Child. Before we reached our destination, "Garden Party" played on the radio, prompting me to talk about Ricky Nelson. I explained that his sons, Matthew and Gunnar, The Nelsons, were coming to town to perform "Ricky Nelson Remembered." That reference evolved into a tale told in stepping-stone fashion which led to naming the puppy.

I had interviewed Ricky in 1985, but an unkind fate would destine that meeting to be his final interview when he perished with several others later that same day. On December 31, 1985, I was conducting brief interviews with celebrities regarding their New Year's Eve plans and New Year resolutions. The scheduled five-minute interview with Ricky turned into a 90-minute discussion from which I felt the foundation of a new friendship. We even made plans to meet the following January at The Royal Palms. A few hours later, I arrived at a party finding many in tears. I immediately called the radio station to have them pull the Ricky Nelson interview only to learn the station planned to air the entire chat. I detest sensationalism and later heard the station managers were more than miffed when I allegedly absconded with the tapes.

The next day, I called my buddy, renowned author, Og Mandino. He agreed to inscribe my favorite of his books to Ricky's mother, Harriet Nelson. As with many of my childhood friends, "The Ozzie & Harriet Show" had been a staple in my TV-viewing diet. Celebrity sleuth that I am, I sent the book directly to Mrs. Nelson's home with a personal note sharing some of the interview with her. Mrs. Nelson would later tell me that Og's *The Greatest Miracle in the World* with "The God Memorandum" was the light which got her through those many dark days. In a time when people wrote handwritten letters, we became regular pen pals and shared occasional phone calls. Mrs. Nelson had a great wit and lovely handwriting I treasured over the next nine years.

During this same time, Matthew and Gunnar took a workshop at Omega Vector where I did (and still study). We never met, however. In recent years, I have come to know and admire Ricky's talented daughter, actress Tracy Nelson, who also is a gifted writer. My soul was warmed when she shared that she was given the book her Grandmother Harriet had kept by her bed. *The Greatest Miracle in the World* now rests on Tracy's nightstand. I also came to know Ricky's youngest son, Sam Hilliard Nelson, while he was producing a DVD collection enhancing the 14 years of the TV series featuring his grandparents, "Ozzie & Harriet."

This chat with fellow *NCIS* fan Duffy led me to mention that Mark Harmon was Tracy, Matthew, Gunner and Sam's uncle. Mark Harmon. Poof! "Gibbs." When I first met this little pup, he stood and smacked another dog on the back of the head. That 'Gibbs-slap' sealed the deal. I had a new dog and a new friend.

Once home, I took a notepad, wrote a vow to my new companion and stuck the note on the refrigerator with a magnet. "*NOTE TO GIBBS: I promise I will never compare you to Nubble, but you will probably hear his name a lot.*" Entering my Word Corner, I discovered almost 200 queries asking if I had come home with a puppy. I posted my simple message on Facebook announcing the arrival of my new four-legged friend. So it began.

This form of messaging turned into a recordation of daily observations of first-time moments that cover the gamut of humor, challenge, seriousness and insight. The notes have become so popular, I receive calls and messages from around the country about the impact that the *NOTE TO GIBBS* concept has on individuals and their families. I realize I am going to have my heart broken again, but hopefully not for quite a few years to come. Meanwhile, I want to fill this little guy's heart with as much love as I can.

Thanks for allowing us to share a part of our journey with you. ~ Pierre O'Rourke, Scottsdale, AZ

Foreword by Laurie Notaro

There are few things more readily able to melt a heart than the furiously wagging behind of a puppy, so anxious to meet and lick the nose of even a perfect stranger. Whether an honest burst of unbridled happiness or a calculated ploy to ensnare a belly scratch or a cookie, the wagging fanny is often the first experience we have when meeting a future companion for the first time. Their excitement becomes our excitement, their love opens the door for our love to run straight to the nearest pet store, buy the comfiest, fluffiest bed, the most dashing collar and, if they're cute enough, a sweater and possibly matching booties.

What is it about the wagging fanny that breaks us down in seconds flat, reverts our regular speaking voices into ones several octaves higher and enables our brains to produce fifteen nicknames in as many seconds? Is it magic, an inane talent for magnetism, or slight of hand that permits us to not exactly see one paw on the couch, followed slinkily by a second, third and then fourth, until sleepy eyes begin to close in your lap? The instant look, worthy of a Method actor, that transforms the snout, implores the eyes and deflates the ears after you've informed them that this is the last treat, making resistance futile in the matter of an encore jerky strip. Don't even try; just hand it over, pally. It's the last one when I say it's the last one!

Honestly, I believe it's nothing short of dog craft, the enchanting ability of a dog to be there whenever we need them, for knowing what we're thinking and the gift of making their farts hilarious, particularly when they are looking for them. How else can you explain the uncanny ability of dogs to tell us pretty much what they're thinking without saying a word, just eliciting a hop, wag or pant, and most of that time, the message is something awfully nice. The unadorned lean-in that makes everything seem just that much better and says, without even a look, that you are so wanted. The nuzzle in the morning that says, "I'm up, so you be up, too!" The paw on the knee that tells you that we are not only friends, but we are partners, too. You for me, me for you. Forever, wherever we go.

Few partnerships could convey that connection more than that of Gibbs and his buddy, Pierre. The dog craft that exists between those two is woven, delightful and cheeky. They travel together, live together, joke together, and take care of one another, despite doggie door mishaps, night time gas attacks, eating poo (rarely on Pierre's part) and toilet bowl play. Pierre's notes to Gibbs are nothing short of Pierre's own wagging tail; the loyalty goes both ways, equally as fierce. It's a fine pairing, as Gibbs, still really a puppy with a wagging fanny himself, tests the waters and Pierre gently but hysterically guides him along, imparting wisdom, advice, and the demand that no matter what, even when good dogs do bad dog things, they still love each other.

Here's my Note to Gibbs, to Pierre and everybody under the spell of dog craft: The love is always there in that wagging fanny; you just have to wag a little back. ~ Laurie Notaro

Disclaimer

No animals were harmed during the writing or publication of this book. The same cannot be said for a pizza, tennis shoe, cheese sandwich, mattress or several dog toys. None of the characters depicted in this work is fictitious. Any resemblance to real persons, dogs, cats or other animals, living or dead, is purely coincidental in that, coincidentally, they are real. No names have been changed to protect the innocent or otherwise, as all this stuff really happened.

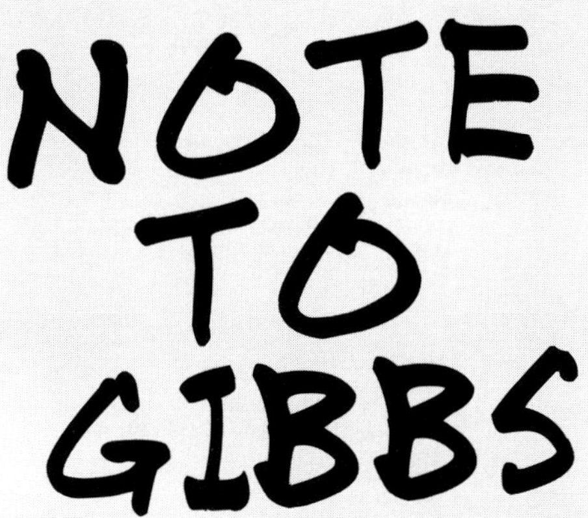
NOTE
TO
GIBBS

NOTE TO GIBBS:

I PROMISE I WILL NEVER COMPARE YOU TO NUBBLE, BUT YOU WILL PROBABLY HEAR HIS NAME A LOT.

DREWAQUILINA2013

NOTE TO GIBBS:

I'M NOT WORRIED ABOUT THE NOSE PRINTS ON THE CAR WINDOW. IN FACT, I KINDA MISSED THEM.

DREWAQUILINA2013

NOTE TO GIBBS:

THAT'S MIRROR DOG.
HE SHOWED UP WHEN YOU
DID AND IS FRIENDLY.
HE ISN'T GOING TO
STEAL YOUR BALL.

DREWAQUILINA2013

NOTE TO GIBBS:

I WAS AMAZED AT YOUR FIRST WALK WITH THE GENTLE LEADER. NO, THE BUNNY RABBITS WERE NOT LAUGHING AT YOU. SOME OF THEM JUST HAVE BAD SINUSES.

DREWAQUILINA2013

NOTE TO GIBBS:

THOSE ARE WIND CHIMES. ALSO OUR FRIENDS. WELL, THEY ONLY SING WHEN THE WIND BLOWS. YOU CAN'T SEE THE WIND, BUT SHE'S FEMALE. THEY CALL HER MARIAH.

DREWAQUILINA2013

NOTE TO GIBBS:

PULLING ON BIJOU'S EAR
WHEN HER EYES ARE CLOSED
IS NOT HOW TO ASK,
"DO YOU WANT TO PLAY?"

DREWAQUILINA2013

NOTE TO GIBBS:

I'M NOT FINDING THE ANSWER IN MY PUPPY BOOK AS TO HOW TO TEACH YOU NOT TO TINKLE ON YOUR OWN FRONT FOOT.

DREWAQUILINA2013

NOTE TO GIBBS:

THANKS FOR REMINDING ME, THROUGH YOUR EYES AND ACTIONS, WHAT IT IS LIKE TO SEE THINGS FOR THE VERY FIRST TIME.

DREWAQUILINA

NOTE TO GIBBS:

RELAX. THE CAR IS NOT SWISHING ITS TAIL AT YOU. THAT'S THE REAR WINDSHIELD WIPER.

DREWAQUILINA2013

NOTE TO GIBBS:

I KNOW IT WAS YELLOW AND IT BOUNCED WHEN IT ROLLED OFF THE COUNTER. BUT DID I SAY 'FETCH?' DID I SAY 'CATCH?' I KNOW I DIDN'T SAY 'BITE IT!' THAT WAS A LEMON. YES, VERY SOUR.

NOTE TO GIBBS
DREWAQUILINA2013
Gibbs

NOTE TO GIBBS:

THE SHUTTERS MAY LOOK LIKE LADDERS, BUT SHUTTERS ARE NOT LADDERS. THIS IS NOT OPEN TO DISCUSSION.

NOTE TO GIBBS:

KEEP YOUR SILLY HEAD OUT OF HER VENETIAN BLINDS. VENETIAN IS FRENCH FOR '**NO!**'

DREWAQUILINA2013

NOTE TO GIBBS:

I SO LOVE TO AWAKEN TO
YOUR LITTLE BLACK NOSE
AND BIG BROWN EYES ...
EVEN THE PUPPY BREATH.

NOTE TO GIBBS:

THESE ARE NOT YOUR TENNIS BALLS; THEY BELONG TO THAT LADY. YES, SHE KNOWS THEY'RE STUCK TO THE BOTTOM OF HER WALKER. I KNOW THEY LOOK BRAND NEW, BUT SHE NEEDS THEM TO HELP HER WALK. I DON'T KNOW; MAYBE HER PUPPY TANGLED HIS LEASH AROUND HER LEGS AND MADE HER FALL.

DREWAQUILINA2013

NOTE TO GIBBS:

EVERYONE REMARKS
HOW SMART YOU ARE,
SO IT WOULD BEHOOVE YOU
NOT TO STICK YOUR HEAD
THROUGH THAT FENCE AGAIN.

NOTE TO GIBBS:

NO, 'BEHOOVE' DOES
NOT APPLY TO HORSEYS.

DREWAQUILINA2013

NOTE TO GIBBS:

BIJOU ISN'T MAGICAL.
IT'S A DOGGIE DOOR.
JUST FOLLOW HER AND
YOU CAN GO INTO THE
BACKYARD. REALLY.
NO, THE DOOR ISN'T
ATTACKING YOU. FINE,
BIJOU IS MAGICAL.

NOTE TO GIBBS:

IT ISN'T A
GUILLOTINE. YOU GOT
YOUR HEAD THROUGH.
NOW JUST GET YOUR
HINDQUARTERS
TO FOLLOW YOU.

DREWAQUILINA2013

NOTE TO GIBBS:

DOING KITTY CAT YOGA STRETCH, VERY GOOD. DOING IT RIGHT IN FRONT OF ME AS I WALK, NOT SO MUCH.

DREWAQUILINA2013

NOTE TO GIBBS:

PIZZAS ARE NOT WAKE-BOARDS
AND THE COFFEE TABLE
IS NOT YOUR OCEAN.

PIZZA
DREWAQUILINA2013

NOTE TO GIBBS:

NO, I DON'T BUY THAT YOU WERE CHECKING OUT THE NEW COUNTERS WHEN MIRROR DOG SHOVED THE TOOTHPASTE TUBE IN YOUR MOUTH.

DREWAQUILINA2013

NOTE TO GIBBS:

PERHAPS I DID NOT MAKE MYSELF CLEAR WHEN I SAID, "NO DIGGING." THAT MEANT IN THE YARD, AT THE DOG PARK AND IN THE FRIGGING BED.

11:17
DREWAQUILINA2013

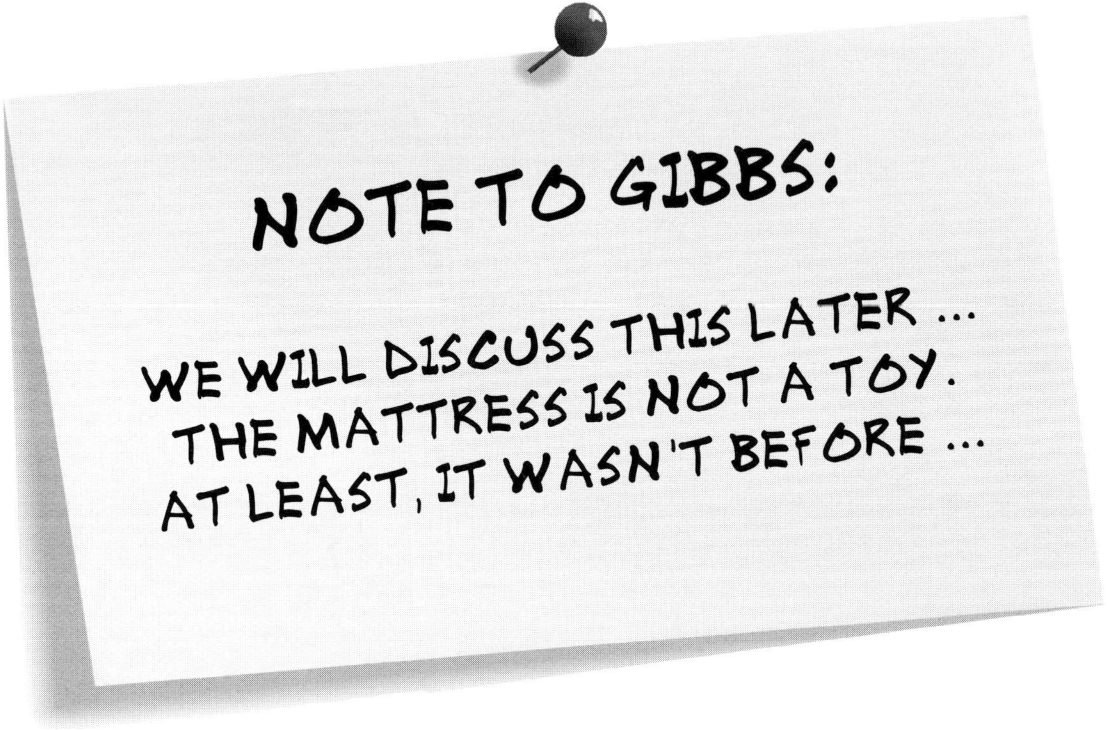

NOTE TO GIBBS:

WE WILL DISCUSS THIS LATER ...
THE MATTRESS IS NOT A TOY.
AT LEAST, IT WASN'T BEFORE ...

NOTE TO GIBBS:

YOU ARE NOT A BAD DOGGIE.
YOU ARE A GOOD DOGGIE ...
WHO DID A VERY BAD THING.
OF COURSE, I STILL LOVE YOU.

NOTE TO GIBBS:

NO, THE BAG OF DOG FOOD IN THE STORE WAS NOT EASILY MISTAKEN FOR A PIÑATA.

PUPPY Food
PUPPY Food
PUPPY Food
PUPPY Food
PUPPY Food
PUPPY Food
DREWAQUILINA2013

NOTE TO GIBBS:

YES, THE NEW SPRINGY THINGS THEY PUT BEHIND THE DOORS DO MAKE A FUNNY SOUND ... FOR THE FIRST TEN MINUTES, ANYWAY.

DREWAQUILINA2013

NOTE TO GIBBS:

I AM SORRY BUT I SAW THE WHOLE THING. MIRROR DOG DID NOT HIT YOU. YOU RAN INTO HIM AND THAT JUST WON'T WORK. BARKING WON'T EITHER. IF YOU INSIST THAT HE KEEPS TAKING THE TOYS YOU WANT TO PLAY WITH, STOP LEAVING THEM NEAR WHERE HE HANGS OUT.

DREWAQUILINA2013

NOTE TO GIBBS:

BIJOU'S FUR IS NOT MADE OF VELCRO.

NOTE TO GIBBS:

NO, WE'RE NOT INSTALLING ASTRO TURF ON THE CEILING TO SEE IF SHE'LL STICK.

DREWAQUILINA2013

NOTE TO GIBBS:

BIJOU'S EAR IS NOT YOUR PULL TOY.
WHEN THE EMPRESS IS SLEEPING,
LEAVE HER ALONE.
REMEMBER ... I WARNED YOU.

DREWAQUILINA2013

NOTE TO GIBBS:

YES, THAT IS DOGGY SHAMPOO
I'M PLACING BY THE SHOWER
BESIDE THREE BIG TOWELS.
WHY DO YOU ASK?

Puppy
Wash
DREWAQUILINA2013

NOTE TO GIBBS:

YOU ARE A GOOD DOG. REALLY. YOU ARE SMART, LOVING AND INTELLIGENT. HONEST. YOU'RE A GREAT DOG. NOW ... WHERE'S MY SHOE?

NOTE TO GIBBS:

GREAT. FOUND MY SHOE. NOW ... LET'S DISCUSS MY CHEESE SANDWICH.

DREWAQUILINA2013

NOTE TO GIBBS:

BECAUSE IF YOU KEEP LICKING IT, YOU'RE GOING TO GO BLIND.

NOTE TO GIBBS:

ARE YOU ACTUALLY ABLE TO FLING YOUR TOYS INTO THE CEILING FAN, OR ARE YOU REALLY AS SURPRISED AS YOU APPEAR TO BE? THIS IS THE FOURTH TIME IN TWO MONTHS - NOT THAT I KEEP COUNT.

NOTE TO GIBBS:

YOUR TOYS GO IN THE TOY BOX,
NOT IN THE TOILET BOWL.
NO, I'M NOT IMPRESSED YOU
FIGURED OUT HOW TO
RAISE THE LID.

DREWAQUILINA2013

NOTE TO GIBBS:

THE TURTLE ISN'T PLAYING HIDE AND SEEK WITH YOU. WELL, I'M SORRY, BUT HE DOESN'T WANT TO INVITE YOU INTO HIS HOUSE.

DREWAQUILINA2013

NOTE TO GIBBS:

WHEELCHAIRS
ARE NOT
AUTOMATIC
LAPS.

DREWAQUILINA2013

NOTE TO GIBBS:

YES, I'M AWARE CELEBRITIES TAKE THEIR 'ESSENCE' AND MAKE COLOGNES & PERFUMES. NO, THAT IS NOT WHAT THE BLUE BAGS ARE FOR.

DREWAQUILINA2013

NOTE TO GIBBS:

I KNOW HE IS A LABRADOR.
I DON'T THINK REFERRING TO
HIM AS A 'BLACK DOG' IS
CONSIDERED BEING
POLITICALLY INCORRECT.

DREWAQUILINA2013

NOTE TO GIBBS:

BIJOU IS GOING TO THE SALON, TOO. YOU'LL BE FINE. NO, THEY ARE NOT GIVING YOU A PERMANENT. I AGREE, THAT WOULD LOOK PRETTY SILLY. BIJOU'S IS NATURAL.

SHAMPOOCH SALON
DREWAQUILINA2013

NOTE TO GIBBS:

HANDSOME ... VERY HANDSOME. YOUR NAILS ARE MUCH SAFER AND NICER, TOO. NO, THEY WERE ALWAYS BLACK. THEY WERE, TOO. NO, THEY DIDN'T DO A GOTH MAKEOVER ON YOU.

NOTE TO GIBBS:

NO, THAT'S NOT A FURRY RAISIN; HE'S A SHAR PEI. NO, HE DIDN'T GET ALL WRINKLY FROM PLAYING IN THE WATER TOO LONG.

NOTE TO GIBBS:

NO, THE COFFEE TABLE
WAS NOT LOWERED.
YOU'RE GROWING.
HOW'S YOUR HEAD?

DREWAQUILINA2013

NOTE TO GIBBS:

KITTY POOPS ARE NOT TOOTSIE ROLLS. I DON'T CARE WHAT BIJOU SAID; SHE WAS KIDDING. IF BIJOU SAID 'JUMP OFF THE ROOF,' WOULD YOU? I DON'T KNOW IF THERE'S A SWIMMING POOL BELOW. NO, WE ARE NOT GOING ON THE ROOF TO LOOK.

DREWAQUILINA2013

NOTE TO GIBBS:

IT IS A PRETTY MOON. THAT'S CALLED A GIBBOUS MOON BECAUSE IT'S A BIT MORE THAN HALF. WELL, IT'S PRONOUNCED 'JIBB' NOT 'GIBB.' I SAW HOW IT'S SPELLED. I DON'T CARE; IT CAN BE A 'GIBB-OUS' MOON THEN. I DON'T KNOW WHERE THEY PUT THE REST OF THE MOON IN THE MEANTIME.

DREWAQUILINA2013

NOTE TO GIBBS:

THAT'S WHAT FROGS DO;
THEY JUMP ... ESPECIALLY
WHEN YOU LEAP AT THEM.
IT DIDN'T HELP THAT YOU
AND BIJOU CHASED HIM
INTO THE HOUSE.

DREWAQUILINA2013

NOTE TO GIBBS:

SO YOU WERE ONLY HOLDING ITS TAIL, AND THE KITTY CAT WAS DOING ALL THE PULLING? OKAY, LET'S GET THE NEOSPORIN.

DREWAQUILINA2013

NOTE TO GIBBS:

WHY IS THE DOOR PERPETUALLY ON THE WRONG SIDE OF WHERE YOU AND BIJOU WANT TO BE?

DREWAQUILINA2013

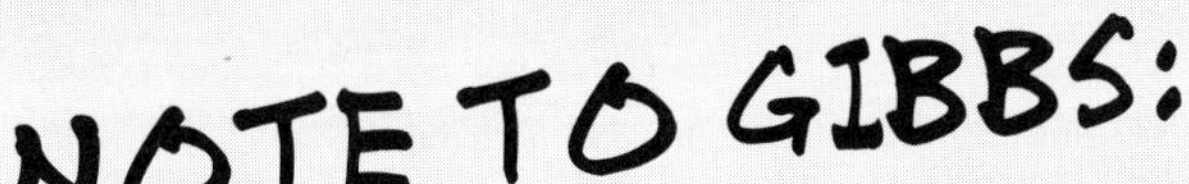

I REALLY DO NOT THINK GOD PLANNED COUNTER HEIGHTS TO MATCH THAT OF A PUPPY ON ITS HIND LEGS.

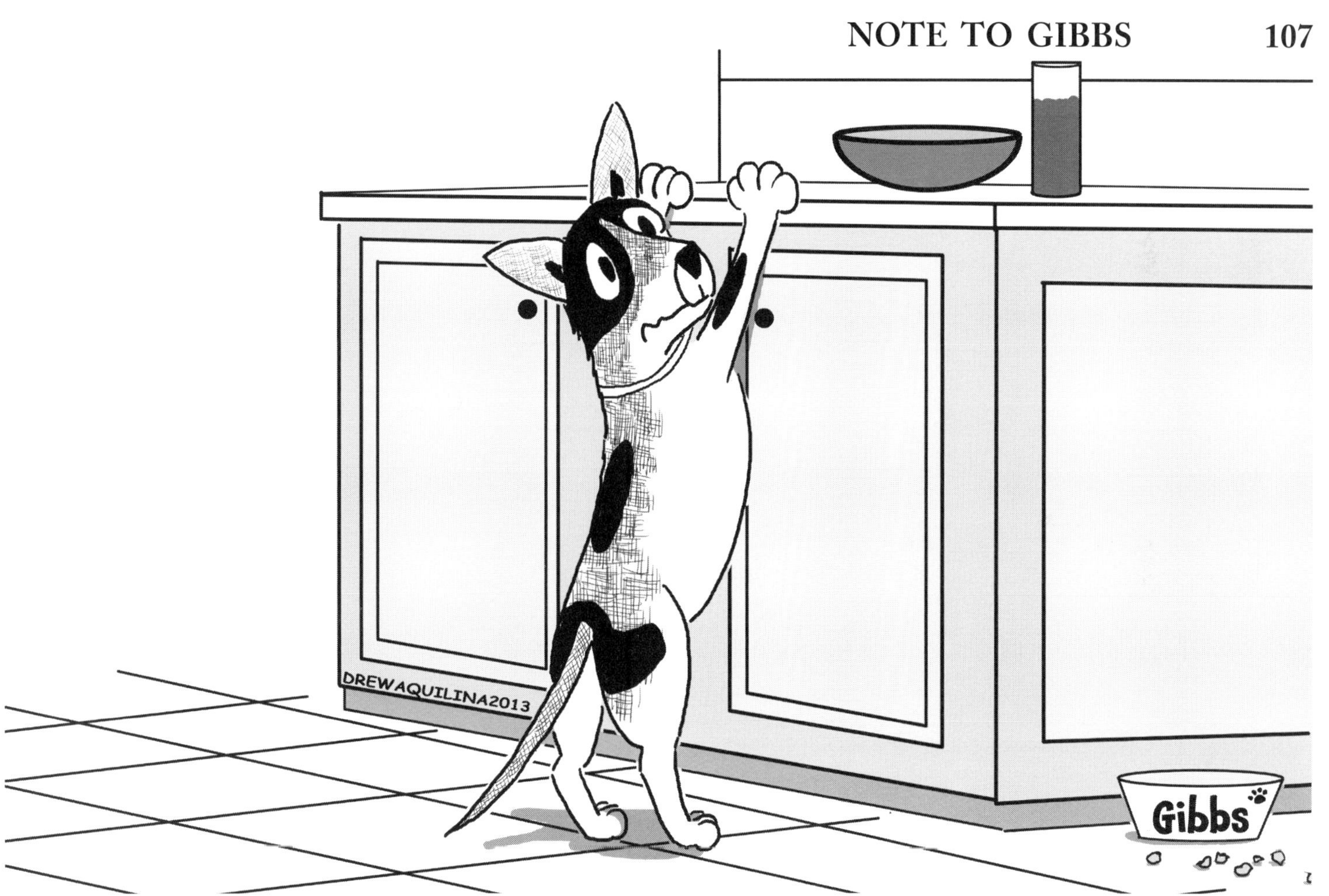
DREWAQUILINA2013
Gibbs

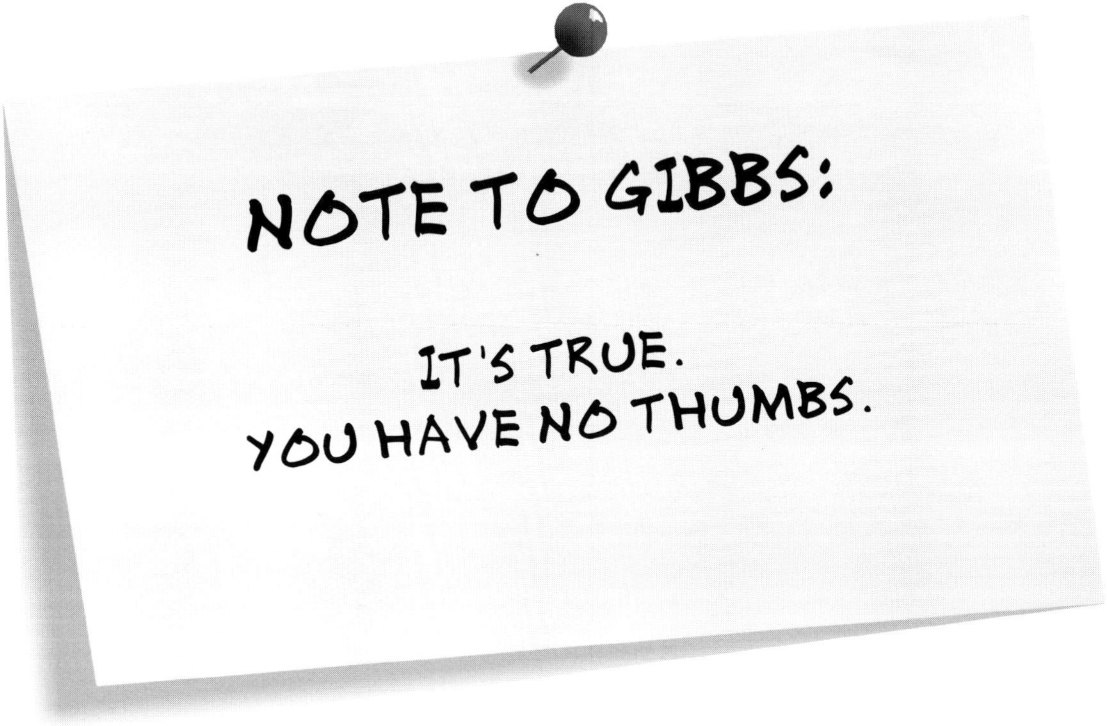

NOTE TO GIBBS:

IT'S TRUE.
YOU HAVE NO THUMBS.

DREWAQUILINA2013

NOTE TO GIBBS:

DUCK POOP IS NOT ONE OF THE
FIVE BASIC FOOD GROUPS.
NO, NEITHER IS KITTY POOP.

NOTE TO GIBBS:

1) DOGGIES ARE NOT ALLOWED CHOCOLATE.
2) TOOTSIE ROLLS ARE MADE FROM CHOCOLATE.
3) STAY OUT OF THE KITTY LITTER BOX.

NOTE TO GIBBS:

THE TREAT BIJOU HAS IS THE VERY SAME KIND YOU HAVE, NO DIFFERENT. YEP, SAME SIZE, SAME FLAVOR. WELL, YOU SHOULDN'T HAVE PUT YOURS DOWN TO GO SNIFF THE ONE SHE HAD.

NOTE TO GIBBS:

ABOUT LAST NIGHT ...
IF THAT WAS ME, WHY
THEN DID IT SMELL LIKE
BLUE BUFFALO DOG FOOD?

04:17
DREWAQUILINA2013

NOTE TO GIBBS:

YOUR LITTLE PUPPY PAW IS
ALREADY THE SIZE OF LILY'S HEAD.
MAYBE IF YOU'D STOP PLACING
IT ON HER HEAD, SHE'D STOP
CALLING YOU GIBBZILLA.

NOTE TO GIBBS:

THAT'S THE ANGELS MAKING THUNDER, HOPEFULLY ANNOUNCING RAIN. OKAY, IF YOU FIGURE THAT'S NUBBLE AND OTHER DOGGIES RUNNING ACROSS THE RAINBOW BRIDGE, THAT'S OKAY, TOO.

NOTE TO GIBBS:

I'M IMPRESSED YOU'VE LEARNED HOW TO DRINK FROM A BOTTLE AND FROM A GARDEN HOSE. HOWEVER, WHEN I'M STANDING IN THE BATHROOM, THAT STREAM IS OFF LIMITS.

DREWAQUILINA2013

NOTE TO GIBBS:

YOU BOTH ARE TIED TO A BALL WASHER SO I CAN RAKE YOUR PAW PRINTS OUT OF THE SAND WITHOUT YOUR HELP. BECAUSE GOLFERS DON'T LIKE DOGGIE PRINTS IN THE BUNKER. I KNOW IT LOOKS LIKE A BIG CAT BOX. NO, I'M NOT EXPLAINING BALL WASHER RIGHT NOW.

DREWAQUILINA2013

NOTE TO GIBBS:

I NEVER NOTICED UNTIL TONIGHT DURING 'NCIS' HOW YOUR EARS PERK UP EVERY TIME ABBY MENTIONS YOUR NAMESAKE.

DREWAQUILINA2013

NOTE TO GIBBS:

I'M GLAD YOU LIKE PLAYING IN THE RAIN AT NIGHT, BUT WHEN GOD BEGINS FLASHING THE LIGHTS, IT'S TIME TO GO INSIDE.

NOTE TO GIBBS:

I'M NOT SURE YOU UNDERSTOOD LAST NIGHT, BUT THANKS FOR PRETENDING YOU DID. SOMETIMES THOUGHTS OF NUBBLE JUST WASH OVER ME. I APPRECIATE YOU WASHING MY CHEEKS WHEN THEY DO.

NOTE TO GIBBS:

I BELIEVE YOU'RE RIGHT.
THAT CROOK IN A PERSON'S
ARM IS JUST PERFECT FOR A
PUPPY TO LAY HIS HEAD.

DREWAQUILINA2013

In Memory of Nubble

Nubble made such an impact in my life and in those of others, the Cattle Herder mix will live on. He came into my life the week I finally succumbed to getting a cell phone and was by my side as I took the leap from occasional penman to author. In his ten years of health, Nubble appeared in numerous magazine articles and two book anthologies, including *The Ultimate Dog Lover*, from which he gained quite the following. He made kids forget what was ailing them and soon will be featured in some children's books. Nubble also continues to live on as the side-kick to 'Daro' in my novels *Free the Puddles* and the upcoming *Driving Me Crazy*. He even has a line of greeting cards soon to be released. Stories including pictures through the ages are presented on my website.

There is not enough room to share all that Nubble meant to me, his antics or the lessons we both experienced. I must mention, however, how Nubble lay long hours in my Word Corner allowing me to bounce ideas off him, befriended a one-legged pigeon I named 'Eileen,' corralled a car thief, turned a man's toupee into a toss toy, swam so much he almost grew gills, never met a Frisbee or ball he didn't like, had a best-friend named Bijou, had Molly and Lily as girlfriends, went with me to a cabin for my birthday treks, and finally, let me know when it was time to take our last walk.

The pup that came into my life a year-and-a-half after Nubble's passing has a large black spot on his right side. We have come to understand it is Nubble's paw print from picking out Gibbs for God to send me. That may be silly, but it's what I choose to believe.